A QUEEN'S ANTHEM

Poetry Anthology Volume II

A QUEEN'S ANTHEM

Poetry Anthology Volume II

Rian N. Jenkins

Copyright © 2021 by Rian N. Jenkins

All rights reserved, including the right of reproduction in whole or in part in any form. No part of this book may be reproduced, stored in, or introduced into a retrieval system, or transmitted, in any form or by any means (electronic, mechanical, photocopying, recording, or otherwise) without prior written permission from the author.

If you purchased this book without a cover, you should be aware that this book is stolen property. It was reported as "unsold and destroyed" to the publisher, and neither the author nor the publisher has received payment for this "stripped book."

ISBN: 978-1-7353316-2-1

Photography by Vic Weaver Photography

Cover Designed by WaveGraphix, LLC

Artwork by April Nealey

Edited by Tamika L. Sims of Get Write with Tamika, LLC

WrightStuf Consulting, LLC

Columbia, SC

www.wrightstuf.com

Published by Rian N. Jenkins

Crowned By Nichele, LLC

For information on the content of this book, email

crownedbynichele@gmail.com

www.riannjenkins.com

Printed in the United States of America

OTHER PROJECTS

A Queen's Heart (Poetry Anthology Volume I)

FUTURE PROJECTS

The Reverse YA Novel Series

LUKE BROWN

The Coronation: A Queen's Devotional

This book is dedicated to all the present and past queens in my life.

From my mother, Barbara Jenkins-Reaves, to my grandmothers, the late Mary Jenkins-Dent and the late Viola Mungin.

From all my aunts and cousins along with family friends, mentors, and teachers.

I have learned to embrace the crown bestowed on me because of you.

Acknowledgments

Because of God, I possess a gift that comes with much responsibility and power. Sometimes I do wish I was more consistent with cultivating my gift and never second-guessing it.

I am thankful to my family and friends who have supported me over the years. I appreciate people who have given me a platform to speak life at their venues and events.

Barbara Ann, I put pen to hand because of the generational blessing passed from your DNA. Hopefully, I will also see you published even if I must do it myself! Most importantly, I learned what it was like to be a queen reigning, being the best of the best. From motherhood, teaching, mentoring, leadership, and even shopping are a few of the areas you execute so well. Excellence is what you do best.

For anyone who was graced by the presence of my grandmothers, the Late Mary Jenkins-Dent and the late Viola Mungin, you know they exemplified royalty. Dignified women people listened to and gleamed from their wisdom. They possessed a heart of gold. With Grandma Ola, she would cook meals filled with laughter. Both of my grandmothers believed in you knowing your history so your future will be successful. They were constantly telling us stories about how my father was able to put himself through school or how God can get through anything in life. They were women of prayer who would constantly reminisce about how good God is. I truly miss them!

I have been blessed with many aunts who treated me like a daughter. Also, I have been blessed with cousins who treated me like a sister. My mom would never hesitate to pass the phone to me so they could reiterate what she already said. With my cousins, they were never afraid to pull me to the side and speak life into me. They carry the same spirit that my grandmothers possessed. I appreciate you being who you are.

Pastor Marcia, my spiritual mother, who continues to pour life into me. You continue to empower me to maximize my Godly potential. Because of you and Bishop, I am awakened to my authority.

My best friends, Wendy Chaplin and Ebony Young who have always been supportive since day one. I can always bounce ideas off of you. I could always laugh and cry with you while being transparent.

Special thanks to Cierra House aka Cierra Blessednda House, Mischa Elise Pugh aka Madame Juice, Tiffany Wider aka TifanyJ, Karen Joyner aka Wintah Storm, and the women of SWATA at Right Direction Christian Church International. You have welcomed me along with encouraging and coaching me. QUEENS SUPPORT QUEENS.

I am greatly appreciative of Tamika Sims who I made

the mistake of dodging for years. I am extremely blessed to work and gleam from you. Your gift, your testimony is a gift empowering many women to pursue their dreams with their pen.

Naomi Moore, the co-designer of my cover, I am so proud of you young queen. Continue to be great!

Jeffrey Guillaume, I am grateful we were able to finally collaborate.

April Nealey, you are an artistic genius who I am elated to have your work included in this project.

Table of Contents

Woke Up Like 3

A Queen's Battle..9

QUEEN PERIODT! 17

Crowned..19

Heaven's Jewel 21

I AM BOLD 25

Queens Don't Bow 31

Wake Up, Silly Women 35

Promise..41

The Process: Have You Met Him? 43

Forever A Queen 47

Shine..49

We Need You..57

I Deserve Better 63

Awaken...69

Must Deny the Lie..73

Destroying the Female Myth 75

But he said 79

Worthy 83

Warrior Queen 91

Woke Up Like . . .

I woke up like this . . .

    not necessarily flawless

Faultless

Clothed in His righteousness.

Covered in favor.

Worthy of every blessing He promised.

Flaws are made perfect in His strength.

Literally Heaven sent.

His majesty, in all His glory and power

    beautifully handcrafted me

    filled me with purpose.

Don't forget man needed us.

With Adam, He saw something was missing.

A queen exercising her commanding presence.

Never second-guessing my calling --

    a gift to be present,

    dominant in any arena God places me in.

Equipped

Qualified

Refuse to believe the lie I am not valued.

Rubies and diamonds envy.

Lilies and roses bow down

    admiring God's masterpiece.

Reigning and reversing curses.

Sometimes I have to rehearse my victories.

Reminding my soul

Confirming with my spirit,

God's got me.

God's got everything under control.

My life He holds,

    Molded from the beginning to the end.

Author and finisher.

Destined to win.

Yes, I woke up like this.

Victim isn't my title.

See I read in the Bible

    Victory is my story.

Not ripping out the mishaps of my chapter.

A testimony to capture your attention, unlock you from your mental prison and encourage you and others

    you too can be an overcomer.

Ain't no stunting or fronting, pretending

    looking like a silly woman

Awakened to my authority.

Destroying any demons who come after me and my seed.

In Him, I live, move, and have my being.

My life, my only function, is to bring glory to the Father.

I woke up, I wake up giving Him praise.

His Name is the only one powerful enough to annihilate the darkness.

I woke up like this...

    the light of this world.

    Illuminating this Earth.

Bringing hope that will never fail.

Prevailing over every circumstance, situation, or trap.

Temporary setbacks don't compare to everlasting glory.

Nothing blocking me.

Unstoppable, I will live to see the goodness of the Lord.

Yes, I woke up like this ...

    Grateful to be in the land of the living.

    Providing an image to keep pushing.

    Never stop believing

    My latter will be greater.

    Manifestation of healing and restoration will come any minute.

    God's miracle.

    God's daughter

    His friend . . .

    who seeks to hear "well done,"

    assured He won't withhold any good thing.

I woke up like this ...

    Confident I am anointed for every appointed moment.

    God will redeem the time

    While I handle His kingdom like it is mine.

My only truth and reason for living

Forever will be singing and thankful

I am His.

A Queen's Battle

January 5, 2006

all the excitement

Of carrying who my relatives had me convinced

was Nadia.

Most of us were proven wrong.

My sister sang a happy song

Finally a nephew!

His body shaped in a perfect J

I had to bestow on him a perfect name

Joshua.

In the stillness of the moment of excitement

I questioned, "God, what am I going to do with a boy?"

What can I teach him?

Doubt creeping in slowly

Then God reminded me,

"He is your blessing,

you are equipped to handle, love, nurture this boy into a man."

Ten years later,

I have the same question

As I watch this brilliant mind

Constantly grow

Honor roll is the norm

Good manners, chivalry is alive and well.

"He's such a great kid."

I constantly hear while watching him

question the world around him.

"Mommy, why do they have to have commercials about erectile dysfunction?"

"Mommy, do some songs and movies have to have cursing?"

"Mommy, can I be an engineer, art teacher, and illustrator?"

"Mommy, why can't God give me my blessings now instead of later?"

The questions never seem to end

Especially since he is inquisitive and knowledgeable about current events.

Daily he sits with me in front of the TV,

every day at 6:30, Lester Holt on NBC

Sometimes shushing him during the broadcasting

Explaining during the commercials,

but today I couldn't wait until the story was over

All too familiar.

Nevertheless, still puzzling him,

"Mommy, why would a police officer do that?"

I had to assure him all cops aren't bad.

Deep inside I'm mad, infuriated I have to explain

why the one enforcing the law is allowed to take it and wring around countless necks,

choking the life out of my people.

Baggy jeans and Tims, seersucker suit with oxfords,

Hoodies or bow ties.

They believe the lie we are all the same

Black skin makes us guilty

Shoot first

Don't ask no questions

Just doing the duty

deadly force was needed

The animal was going to kill

Or the animal needed to be killed.

Afraid of the jungle or open season

Has them trigger happy.

Again, God, what do I teach my son?

He is a king

Royalty is his namesake.

God created him to reign

Dominate

In the image of perfection

Wonderfully made into a

Conqueror

Warrior

Empowered to handle anything

Yes, we are covered by the blood of Jesus Christ.

The Almighty has His hands on him and me.

His name literally means, "Jehovah saves."

Refusing to believe he is a statistic with two strikes already against him.

Single-parent household and melanin

Others deem as a target.

He is hope, the future, and everything that is right with the world.

Built from purpose and greatness.

No one has the power to stop, block your dreams.

But I would be naive to believe we are invisible to persecution and tragedy.

Life is so precious.

It can be gunned down like it is meaningless.

Before being questioned, arrested...

assumed guilty due to their ignorance.

Others are arrested without incident,

bulletproof vest and a trip to Burger King.

While we, he, she found dead in the streets...

While they lie on the police report they were threatened

by a human who bleeds like them.

Paralyzed by the misconceived notion

We are peasants.

Kings and queens we are!

We shouldn't have to claim our seeds from a morgue

to only have my broken heart to be taped back together with condolences, never solved cases, botched investigations,

Justice becoming a distant relative or nonexistent in some cases.

Settlements can't replace your child.

What will I teach him, God?

When he is frustrated?

Don't get tired of the process.

Trust and believe in change

Despite our ancestors who fought for the same things,

Equalities then seemed like an unattainable dream

Yet, some died or still living with the scars of overcoming the system

That still hasn't quite yet evolved.

When he is angry

he has been questioned, shunned, again without cause

Be respectful

Know your rights.

Don't let your pride shorten your life.

When he wants to be hopeless,

tired of the endless hashtags

left alone with no justice.

I must remind him our hope isn't built on nothing less

Than Jesus Christ and His righteousness.

Not of this world's system

So we must pray, seek wise counsel, believe,

take action,

Pray, seek wise counsel, believe,

take action

Not let my dream turn into a nightmare

Not let my imagination morph into anxiety.

Remembering June 4, 2006, when I held him

Forgetting about the fear of how

Overflowing with gratefulness on why God chose me

To raise this prince into a king

QUEEN PERIODT!

I'm a queen PERIODT!

No, I'm not delirious.

Just made aware of my worth

heavenly, transcending the universe.

Created with a price

Outweighing any regrets, mistakes, pain, or shame.

Nothing will taint my name.

Hard for you to comprehend.

Crowned since birth.

I walk this Earth with elegance and purpose.

Impacting this world with my presence.

Uplifting others.

Rising above stereotypes and lies.

Strutting in the truth

    I will and always be a queen and you are too.

I don't need to prove I am better than you.

Equals . . .

Running our own race

At our own pace.

Rooting on each other.

The goal is for us all to win.

Shining brightly

Inviting all to embrace their crown

Despite how this world, life

Tries to bring you down

Reign proudly PERIODT!

Crowned

I am

A queen.

Royalty is my bloodline, my heritage.

Excellence flows through me.

Who am I to act like

He didn't tattoo my name on His back.

Lashes reaffirming His love for me,

unconditional, unmerited,

Resurrected so I would have no excuses.

Live out my purpose.

Defying and reversing all the curses.

Exerting dominion and power.

My hours are well spent

glorifying the One

whom I live, move, and have my being.

I am the daughter, little goddess,

putting relationship over-promise.

Not seeking stuff, things, and riches.

Focused on His agenda.

Kingdom assignments I will follow.

No longer hollow.

He makes me whole.

My life He controls.

My world He holds.

Nothing, but the best.

Trials, tests, and hardships won't cloud my judgment.

He is the greatest and greatly to be praised.

My sacrifice, my life

Submitted to honoring Him.

Heaven's Jewel

God saw something was missing

Man needed me.

A Queen to reign with my King.

Dominating,

influencing the wind and the seas.

Bringing glory and honor

to the one who created me, us.

Somehow it got lost in transition

The definition of a woman, to some,

    has been diminished.

Some believe the image of who I represent

    is lower than a peasant.

Sit pretty, cute while men ogle over me.

Can't break a nail or mess up my make-up.

Don't think;

    they like it better when I twerk and shut up.

Docile, inferior,

Bending to waves I am meant to train

Answering to names my father never gave me.

Conforming to a system imprisoning potential,

the greatness locked in.

I was told it is not my place.

"You are to be seen and not heard."

Well, I'm forgetting what I learned.

The world had me blind to my crown,

    swimming in mediocrity,

    not realizing my value is unmatched.

Diamonds and rubies laugh nervously,

    jealousy consumed.

They want to emulate me.

Holding my head high.

Never questioning why

    I deserve to wear this crown.

Rocking this crown boldly.

No longer dimming the light

    God created for the world to see.

Breaking all stereotypes.

Making believers out of the naysayers.

Stacking paper taller than skyscrapers.

My invention, best seller, fashion label, restaurant, and

    television network will create multiple streams of wealth.

Blessing all those around me including myself.

Don't throw dirt on my sister.

I give her a ladder to move higher.

Edifying her spirit.

There is no competition.

We all win!

In the midst of the victories, I am tested.

Strengthened through the storms I keep facing.

Tears fall but my faith is unwavering!

Hope keeps me standing.

Forever landing in the promises.

There is no alternative

> when his blood shed for my faults, not his.

Overwhelmed by blessings.

Can't live my life beneath the standard.

The tattoo marks on his back are

> a measure of how great his love is.

Abundance, wealth, prosperity is the language

> I only speak in every aspect of this life's journey.

Never to repeat the lies the world fed me.

God saw something was missing.

Man needed me.

A Queen to reign with my King.

Dominating,

influencing the wind and the seas.

Bringing glory and honor to the one who created me, us.

This world can't truly function with us living on purpose.

I AM BOLD

I am

BOLD

Beautiful Overcomer Living Divinely

in my purpose.

Breaking stereotypes and curses.

Legacies will continue or start with me.

A queen must reign.

Not about knowing my name.

Knowing I sparked change.

Impacted those around me to declare

I AM

BOLD!

No longer being choked

by the world's definition of beauty.

My father's masterpiece.

Makeup or lashes are an accessory, not a necessity.

Carefully, wonderfully, intentionally handcrafted in His image to be a representative.

Mirror love, greatness, excellence

in a world seeking to stifle my potential.

No competition when I follow the calling and plan He set out for me.

My place is etched in stone,

solid rock on which I stand declaring

I AM

BOLD!

Brightly Outshining Lies and Deceit.

Driven to take advantage of every Godly orchestrated opportunity.

No limits.

No sickness, no illness will prohibit me living abundantly.

Those stripes He endured for me

guaranteed I am whole.

Deliverance can happen suddenly or I have to endure the storm longer than desired, the ending result will always be living proof.

I AM

BOLD!

My past is not a deterrent.

Who my mother or father wasn't will not determine I was always born into royalty?

A queen despite my mistakes.

My worth outweighs any naysayers.

Gladly welcoming my haters to the table

to watch me feast on all these blessings

so they can agree

I AM

BOLD!

Blessed, Outstanding Leader of Dopeness!

Brilliantly Original Loving Daring

fine with being an outsider.

Igniting the flame within all

Reminding them of their calling,

their true purpose.

Crowned by His majesty

who paid the price for you and me.

Overcomers, more than conquerors

declaring

I AM

BOLD!

Queens Don't Bow

Queens always

have their heads held high

Recognizing the greatness

Illuminating the soul

Causing the world

to know royalty is gracing their presence.

Marking her territory

Exhibiting the authority

she was given by her Father in Heaven.

Within her inner circle,

Heirs and heiresses to the throne

Only ones who will edify,

help build the kingdom.

Commoners or hecklers are not welcomed.

Allowed within miles of her virtue.

Unless she seeks to help

awaken them to their lineage, importance.

Valuing her legacy.

She isn't foolish

to give her heart to anyone.

Chivalry is irrelevant

if he isn't exercising his dominion

already acknowledging

she is more precious than rubies and diamonds.

Desiring nothing more than to

esteem her higher

than the earth and the stars.

The universe is her playground

Most importantly

A legacy is the constellation

for many nations behind her to

carry on and take to a newer height.

Might or can't isn't spoken

when God's plan is confessed daily.

Surely, goodness and mercy

are the twins that carry her train.

Her name is victory.

Wake Up, Silly Women

Seduced is such a strong word,

an easy escape

placing blame on the predator

devaluing myself to prey.

Prey says I am unintelligent

to think for myself.

All the smoke choking the life out of me.

Forsaking my destiny.

It wouldn't be this way

if I truly treasured myself

at the infinite worth

God created me with.

Instead of devaluing

a Master's piece

lower than peasant change.

Choosing to answer

to a name degrading

denouncing my crown

Stop cracking under the pressure

of loneliness and desperation

Filling a void with emptiness

Never feeding the soul

with what it really needs.

Fellowship with my Savior

who will never disappoint,

fail or leave me to famish.

His grace, His love is sufficient.

I have tasted and seen how good it is.

This is a hunger, a thirst that can´t be neglected.

Forsaking His goodness is like starving to death.

Life is meaningless without Him.

A branch being tossed in the wind,

    With no direction.

    No connection

Eventually being crushed by

the pitfall of this world's promises.

No longer making excuses.

With His power, I can choose

to flee and not succumb to the enemy.

Running into the arms of my Father,

the one who strengthens me to overcome.

Trampling the snakes and scorpions.

On the cross, I already won.

Gold medal status

Being a victim is my past.

Drafted to a team called victory.

Elite and trained to conquer daily.

I can't subject myself to incompetence.

Slaying giants like they are ants.

Ain't nothing I can't do

Abiding in me as I rule

Reigning in His name

Domination flows through my veins.

Lame it is to deny the authority He gives me.

Must operate as the queen and priestess

He called me to be.

Living life and living it abundantly.

Defeat should only be experienced by my enemy.

Fully clothed for battle.

I will stand my ground,

Buckled in truth,

I will never lose.

Because He lives in me,

I am free to speak life.

Making things right.

Manifesting His words.

Bringing the covenant into fruition.

Dispelling darkness.

Illuminating light.

The fight within me will no longer be silenced.

I got it.

I won't block my blessings.

Swimming in the overflow

Rocking the inheritance

Blessed to be a King's kid.

Promise

Too many young mothers' faces

    stuck on the pages of Obituaries

    rather than in the gaze of their children.

Trending tragedies . . .

    My fate couldn't repeat.

I knew in my soul this was temporary.

Prayers of the righteous

    going forth stopped death from coming forth.

All I could envision was my son's face.

Then I looked at Jesus,

    God, my Creator, and Sustainer.

    My Healer who has never forsaken me.

Promise keeper and provider.

I must live this life for Him with fire.

Establishing His kingdom

Dispelling darkness, proving Satan to be heartless, a liar.

I will use this chance to live boldly.

Unapologetically, fearlessly.

No more settling for mediocrity.

No distractions will deter me, prolong me

    from embracing His will for me.

I am His.

Bought with a price.

Eternally, I am indebted, covered by His blood.

Elevated out of the fire and water,

    crowned His daughter.

Called to a purpose greater than

what this Earth gives.

Stagnation will no longer be rehearsed.

Still have more curses to reverse.

Chosen to usher more into His presence.

Prevailing, thriving, advancing in Him.

The Process: Have You Met Him?

There is this guy I want to tell you about.

Some of you have met him and honestly

He is so aggravating but necessary for growth.

His name is the process.

Yes, you must deal with him if you want the promise.

We have this love/strongly distaste relationship

At the end of our encounters, I am blessed

beyond my wants, dreams, and desires.

My heart is overflowing.

Nevertheless, he always has to stress

to experience the inheritance

I must go through him.

Impatient

I want it to fall out of the sky like it says in Malachi.

He laughs

Scoffs at my plea

Must deem myself ready

God made me worthy.

Am I ready to dive deep into the overflow?

The process, he ensures this

so I sit, wait, learn, endure lessons and heartache

Watching others get blessed with what I have been praying for.

I am supposed to rejoice

Say I'm next in line

But as time continues to pluck me on my shoulder

Another boulder of frustration is hurled

afflictions making me want to quit

Forget

He said this is temporary

Just stick with him and the glory that shall be revealed

Won't compare to him.

Keep pressing and stop second-guessing

if it is worth it.

Rushing it only prolongs it.

Remember the last time

Came out shining brighter than the purest gold and diamond

So I will run this race, stay this course with him in my face

Remembering I vowed to no longer become complacent

Royalty I am

No longer settling for the scraps because I am afraid of him, the process.

I am equipped for this journey

Must get everything He has for me.

Every badge, stripe, and scar is an honor

Proof

My God's Word is truth

It cannot lie

Hanging with this guy, the process

will only reveal more excellence, greatness.

A legacy for multiple generations.

I can't forsake Him

My destiny is intertwined with Him

I will stop the whining

Because in actuality, I'm winning.

Forever A Queen

I was

I am

I will forever be a queen

Forget what you heard or witnessed

Forever a queen of the Most High

who never saw me without my crown.

Remembering past actions, decisions, mistakes, mishaps,

hard for you to grasp the notion royalty is my namesake.

Foolish I was to denounce my crown.

Running to fit an image never tailored for me.

A puzzle piece never made to fit into this world.

Saying proudly, I am a daughter of Zion.

Maximizing every gift.

No longer wasting time

The plan must be executed.

Failure is never an option.

Excellence is only accepted.

The tears I let fall due to rejection,

not making the best decisions, losing or coming in second.

Not winning will no longer cloud my judgment.

Refused to be deceived, I am unworthy of the gold place finish.

Lessons to be learned.

Preparing for my victory that has already been won for me.

I have to believe, always push for mastery.

The promises are mine.

More than equipped, so I have to shine.

My God has my back all the time.

A queen,

His queen.

Forever and always.

Shine

It is easy to allow

cuts and bruises

wounds from abuse

misuse of power

to make you feel lower.

Dirt isn't jealous of your position

It is easy to allow

Daddy was never proud

Mother wasn't there

Grandma didn't care

Aunts and uncles weren't aware.

The black sheep feels sorry for you.

It is easy to allow

kids who are so cruel

Picking, teasing, bullying

Rumors and lies

to tie a bow around your life

Have you sitting pretty

Empty

Wrapped in ribbons

Better known as bondage

Unable to walk in your purpose

Aching for the shame

to go away

Nevertheless

Untying the bow seems lame

Not realizing you are playing

into the game of the enemy

Settling for a life

Filled with strife

Eternal life is freely given

A gift to set you free

from your misery

Your spiritual prisons

Unlocked for you

live out your potential

Riches is only a small part of the promise

Having all power

to advance God's kingdom

Using your gift

Your calling to win souls

Inspire and give hope

President Obama isn't meant to be the first and the last.

Some of you are meant to eradicate all of the Hall of Famers' records.

Actors and actresses gracing the red carpet in your threads.

MTV, VH1, BET and YouTube rotating your video that preaches the Gospel

Whatever the wish

Whatever the desire

God wants to ignite a fire

Using you for His glory

Don't let your story

be dictated

by the one who is mad

he can't be you.

Don't be fooled,

tricked or hoodwinked

that throwing back shots

It is not WORTH YOU!

Dropping it like it is hot

then allowing another one to attach

their soul to you is

not WORTH YOU.

Puffing and passing

Poisoning your body with any trash

is not WORTH YOU.

Failure, mediocrity, and stagnation isn't part of your DNA.

Settling C's isn't an option

You can do all things through Christ.

Honor roll is automatic.

You were fearfully and wonderfully made

by the Father

who made you

Kings and Queens

to reign, dominate.

He knew there would be abuse

He knew they would pick on you

He knew you would be neglected by those

who are supposed to protect you.

He knew the lies and rumors would bruise

And He still chose you.

Equipped you to be great

You are not a mistake

The master's plan had you in mind

before He said, "Let there be light."

Start SHINING.

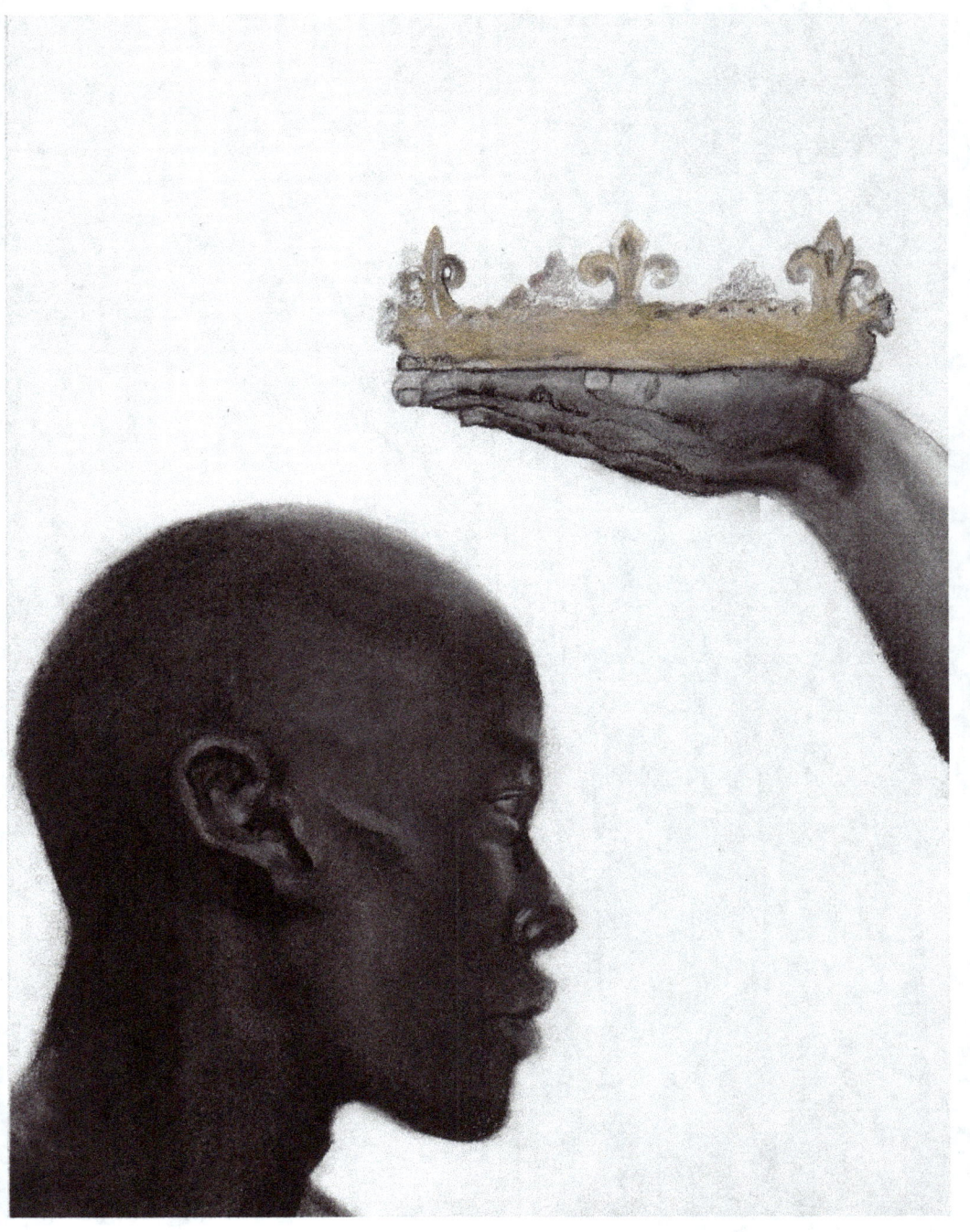

We Need You

Jill Scott wrote a song expressing

there is no second-guessing

we need you.

Life is meaningless without you.

The world is chaos when you are not standing at your throne.

Alone, your queens cannot orchestrate the plan God has for us.

Together, we

create

invent

dominate

generate multiple streams of wealth

Giving back to your community

Empowering others to follow our lead

Again, you are a leader

Intellectual

who will have Bill Gates wanting to partner with you.

Whether it is owning a legit business

Making it into the league

Creating your own label, music or apparel

The world is yours.

Destined for greatness

Your namesake is success.

I don't care about your past.

Your dad may have not been there

Your mom maybe doesn't care.

The streets are all you know.

Society seemingly doesn't offer second chances.

I don't care about the statistics or what is listed on your record.

Despite what you have done

Despite what was done to you

You were created to experience only the best God has for you.

Your priors or any bad decisions

doesn't disqualify you from the promise of wealth and riches.

There is no guarantee it will be easy

It will be worth the journey.

Be willing to fight for what is rightfully yours.

Where you are not doesn't define you or belong to you.

You are and have always been . . .

Intelligent

Innovative

Courteous

Talented

Protective

Passionate

Responsible

Spiritual

Philosophical

Loyal

Genuine

Compassionate

Selfless

Brave

Driven

Confident

KINGS

Again, we need you

on your throne

We can't change the world alone.

I Deserve Better

I deserve better.

Never would I mention or let those words

come out of my lips

at age nine, 11, 12, or 15. Maybe I had the hopes and dreams

you would get your life together.

Love me,

devote your life to me.

Make sure I had everything I need,

which was YOU.

Instead of smoking weed --

Your best friend and your daughter.

Neglecting me to

have a puff of the smoke

that would carry you away

from what I don't understand

Daddy, I am yours

and you are mine.

Yet, I feel like an old toy forgotten under the bed, dusty and dirty.

Was I stressing you out that much

being a father wasn't a priority.

Cleaning yourself up

should be your mission.

I can't comprehend

How I wasn't enough?

I deserve better

Didn't ask to be here

Yet I sit and watch you

waste your life away

Hoping and praying

you will eventually say

I am done

Apologizing for all your wrongs.

Seeking to only cause me to forget

Causing my fantasy to be a reality

Shouting to the world

"That's my daddy."

Maybe you were never taught

How to nurture

The absence of your father

has you mistakenly believing

what you give is good enough

Wasted potential.

Should be out getting a job,

But yet you are laying up here.

Collecting a check.

I say I deserve better.

Only in head

Again at the age of age nine, 11, 12, or even 15

I couldn't utter these words

Tobe engulfed in wanting to truly be "Daddy's girl"

Your pride and joy.

Hearing Marvin Gaye and Stevie Wonder

Imagining you are singing their songs to me.

Got glimpses here and there

when you would hug me and kiss me

and say, "I love you."

Taking me shopping every blue moon.

Not realizing I can't forget . . .

being picked up late or not being picked up at all.

Not showing up

Practices

Recitals

Awards ceremonies

You said you would be there.

You were not always there.

You would think I would be used to broken promises.

Clinging on to hope like it is my lifeline.

Declining the notion it will always be this way.

I deserve better

Please now . . .

Give me better

I am willing to forgive the latter

Focus on the future

Willing to move forward

If you are willing to give me better.

No, I will never abandon you.

I will always love you.

I deserve that father figure

that I was born to have.

Please give me better.

Awaken

Satan speaks lies and demons never sleep

Seeking to keep me imprisoned

from maximizing my potential

Polluting my mind

Poisoning me to believe

I am unworthy

Settling for the world's definition of greatness,

MONEY, SEX, and POWER

fit into the equation.

I get mine

Not worrying about you

or my seeds that are at risk

to repeat the same generational curse

overtaking me.

Delusional

Empty

Unhappy

I find myself in the sanctuary

Crying out to the only God

who can save me.

Deliver me from this bondage.

Erase all my shame

Bestowing my original name

QUEEN

Equipping me for battle

Victorious

Unstoppable

Unmovable

Unwavering

Satan is still speaking lies

The demons never sleep

Dumbfounded

I can't be

defeated

deceived

manipulated

to conform again

to a system only meant

to disarm me.

Destroy me

Fully aware of my authority

and the power that dwells within

Strengthen to always win

Impossible doesn't mean anything.

Failure is never an option

Wised up to his deception.

It is in Christ I live, move, and have my being.

He transforms my thinking

Reminding me constantly

Abiding in Him

Enables me to receive

Abundance

Overflow

Peace

Prosperity

Planted like a tree

bearing fruit for all to taste and see

that the Lord is good.

Greatly to be praised

For the rest of my days

I will declare how awesome He is

Living out my purpose in Him

Being a witness

Deliverance is real

Awakening others from their comatose state

Giving you the antidote,

the truth . . .

You don't have to believe

the lies Satan keeps telling.

You don't have to hide from the demons who never sleep.

Reclaim your throne

Use your sword to cut their throats

Dismantling the kingdom of darkness.

Must Deny the Lie

Can't deny the lie resurfacing from time to time:

It is okay to love you,

    need you,

    want you.

You never even left the glass half empty.

Too busy leaving holes draining my soul.

Drenched in tears

Promises to love me were never fulfilled.

Leaving me cold like a nice child on Christmas morn'

who ends up with the bag of switches and coal.

Undeserving of this bull, garbage.

I set fire to every broken record to warm my soul.

Refusing to die and now relive this lie it is okay to

love you,

    need you,

    want you.

Destroying the Female Myth

What is uplifting, empowering

about calling myself or my fellow sister

a female dog?

Even with the meanest, nastiest attitude

with the tendency of being rude,

why must I equate my worth

to a pet who can be trained to play fetch?

Yeah, I'm running things by having dreams to take over …

one of the next Fortune 500 Companies

the fashion and entertainment industries

the school district by being superintendent.

I might decide to write a book about

how I overcame all obstacles

while steering clear of the myth

that I, a queen, am on the same level

of a female terrier or French poodle

who will do all sorts of tricks to get a treat.

I realize my temple is worth more than

any dollar amount you can think of.

Once you think you added up the figures,

I would have to tell you

to add some more zeroes.

Besides, I don't need you to toss me

goodies to push me along my journey.

I already have a Captain

steering in the right direction with added blessings.

Authoritative I am,

I will execute the master plan

not requiring a man

to hold my hand or

have me locked and chained inside a fence.

He is afraid of a little competition.

The One who created me

gave me all the power I need to fulfill destiny.

He also helped me to believe

I am made in the image of perfection

dispelling the myth of being content with

someone making it positive

to be called a female dog.

But he said . . .

But he said

    I love you.

Three words I have never heard

have me frozen for a moment.

Desperation to keep me

has him screaming words

he doesn't know the meaning.

Tears streaming,

crying a river intentionally.

Chasing safety.

I am his lifesaver.

I have snatched that S off my chest

to show him my heart

is still bleeding

through the bandages

he used to patch with those three words.

But he said

    I love you.

My silly nature wants to melt.

Forget all the promises and lies

I have been dealt.

No longer willing

to play the fool.

I remind him

he chose to run the streets,

take her home,

left me alone wondering

again if she is really *just* a friend.

Interactions I witnessed contradicted your truth,

piling up to garbage I seek to burn.

You know fire too well.

Burning my trust countless times.

Nothing rises from your ashes, but dirt and dust.

But he said

    I love you.

A must to have you in my life

I once felt.

Stressing,

not willing to grasp the notion

your mess is finally pushing me out the door.

Frantic,

singing this song

you can't recognize the melody.

Pretending to care

when you are scared

the best thing ever happened to you

has my keys in my hand.

Making amends wasn't tonight's motives

Clearly you forgot

I said I am not,

can't and won't

play this game with you any longer.

Yet you try to win me over

AGAIN.

Apprehensive

then remembering my vow

to not be in denial any longer.

Even the most delirious person

can see you don't or will ever love me.

Worthy

As I look in the mirror

reflections of the past flash me back

to nights I wasted smashing the next one

not caring about the generational curse overtaking me

tainting a Master's piece

only meant for perfection in Him

edification and glorification of Him.

Flaws are permitted to be eventually

acknowledged …

mended …

forgiven …

repented of …

and atoned of …

washed in the blood.

Nevertheless,

those same flaws want to resurrect

leaving my mind, soul, and Spirit battling for life.

Life, not death, is my choice.

To walk in my purpose.

Errors in judgment whisper over my shoulder

Seeking to reverse my thinking...

Wanting me to forget

I have been healed,

bandaged scars are no longer visible.

Now mistakenly want to view myself

as damaged goods.

Causing me to think I am not worthy to

be a representation of His glory.

People can't take you seriously.

Fearing what could possibly be.

Assuming failure will be my constant demise.

Then I lift my eyes to the hills

from which comes my help.

Hearing . . .

I am an overcomer

More than a conqueror

Empowered to do everything

He called me to do and be.

Greater is He who is within me.

A new creature,

all things have passed away

Forgiveness and repentance are the doorway

to the sea of forgetfulness

where I can swim with no regret.

Persevering to the next dimension in Him.

Remembering He only has plans for me to prosper.

Making me worthy of the honor of being called His daughter,

heir to an inheritance

going further than multiple bank accounts.

Generational wealth-producing blessings for others to savor

Proceeding me is favor while grace and mercy follow me

on this journey destined for greatness

My name is on it!

He created me for this moment

for this lifetime of abundance.

Breaking through all barriers

Reversing the curse

Trailblazing a legacy to be passed on to countless generations.

Springing forth the message

everyone representing the Father truthfully

is worthy of every single dream,

Godly designed wish, plan

to be granted and brought into fruition.

No longer second-guessing this forgiven Christian

isn't worthy

when He died on the cross for me,

went down to hell snatched the keys,

unlocking me from my cell in the penitentiary of sin.

No, I am not a fugitive.

A redeemed soul who has the right

to abundant life,

which isn't limited to riches.

Being used as an instrument to resound loudly,

"God so loved the world that He gave his son.

Yes, He loves you that much!"

or

"If He healed and restored,

this once broken girl who is

now this whole woman you now see,

what more could He do for you?"

Remembering before the foundations were laid

He called my name

Fearfully and wonderfully

making me worthy

before any mistakes were made.

Knowing sin would make sin my temporary fix

He died to erase the shame

declaring it was finished

Making me worthy.

I am worthy

I am worthy

I am worthy

This confession will pour out of my lips

whenever doubt creeps in.

Never will I believe the lie the devil speaks

seeking to stifle me.

Determined to carry out the assignment

Advancing my Father's Kingdom

A force causing all demons to flee

Exercising my authority

Declaring the truth

I am and will forever be

worthy.

Warrior Queen

Stilettos and Chucks are the make-up

of this warrior queen

who has stepped on the scene

using the mic

as a device to speak life.

Yes, this flow will be different.

Ripping this track with my poetic essence.

You can call me Anointed Misfit.

Confident

the elegance of my words will take you higher.

Lighting a fire in your soul.

Setting you free from the lies the devil told.

Speaking rhymes that only resurrect.

Reminding you that your old man is dead.

Declaring you possess all power

to walk out your purpose.

Failure and stagnation isn't an option.

Killin' them demons is part of our assignment.

Expanding God's Kingdom.

Slaying the kingdom of darkness.

Yes, I do all this...

After all, I am His instrument!

An instrument

who doesn't want you to forget

your life is precious, priceless.

Don't be naive to the devil's devices.

Alcohol, greed, drugs, sex, violence

is quickly silencing, destroying, killing

who God only meant

for you to experience life

more abundantly.

No, it's not lame.

Trust me I have seen both sides of the game

Glad to declare I will ride or die

for Christ.

Tasted and saw,

refusing to be lost

when the way has been drenched

with blood that should have been my own.

Yet, he showed how much he loved me.

Erasing my inability

to recognize the King who reigns.

Still making me one with Him.

How can I turn my back on Him?

I am supposed to be dead,

but here I stand.

Blessed to be a blessing.

Victorious living.

Rocking the mic for Jesus.

About the Author

Rian N. Jenkins' has been in love with writing since sixth grade. Close to thirty years, she has inspired, entertained, and educated many through poetry, novellas, journalism, and performances. Finally, she can add author to her resume. Along with being a gifted writer, she has been a middle school teacher for seventeen years.

She is the mother of Joshua. In her spare time, she loves to watch sports, especially football, thrift, and read a lot of YA lit she shares with her students and the world via YouTube.

Check out her website, WWW.RIANNJENKINS.COM

www.ingramcontent.com/pod-product-compliance
Lightning Source LLC
Chambersburg PA
CBHW071903070526
44583CB00016B/1826